The Deer Report

Contents

Chapter 1
School

Kelsey did not want to go to school.
Usually she was excited about
the first day of school.
Not this year.
She did not want to go to school.
Kelsey did not want to leave
the little fawn she called Baby.

Goldie, Kelsey's dog, had found the
fawn shivering under the porch.
The fawn had lost its mother
and was cold and frightened.
Kelsey had been taking care of the
fawn ever since Goldie found him.

Josh was at the bus stop.

Josh was Kelsey's friend
from next door.

He was the veterinarian's son.

"You don't look very happy,"
Josh said to Kelsey. "How come?"

"I don't want to go to school.
I don't like leaving Baby,"
Kelsey replied.

"Goldie and your dad
will look after the fawn," Josh said.

"I know," said Kelsey.
Both Goldie and Kelsey's dad would
be there to look after the fawn.

Chapter 2
Mrs. Vince

When they got to school,
Kelsey and Josh walked
down the hall
to Mrs. Vince's
second grade classroom.
Mrs. Vince stood in the doorway.
"Find your name tags
and take a seat,"
she said to Josh and Kelsey.
Kelsey and Josh looked around.
They found their desks
and sat down.

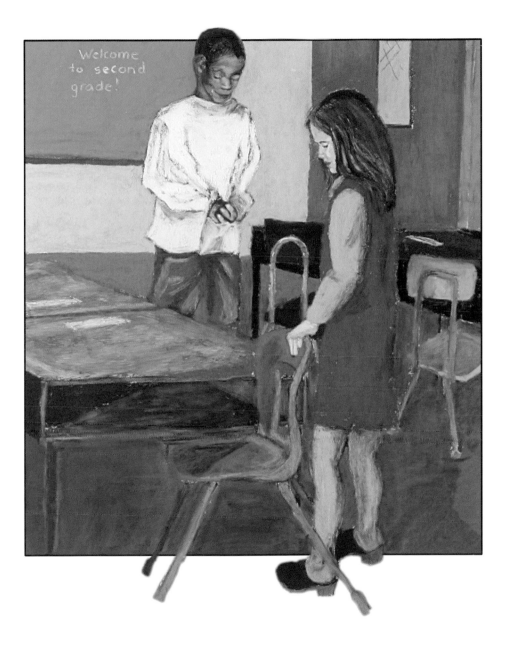

"Second grade is a very
important year,"
Mrs. Vince said.

Mrs. Vince took out some paper.
"Now, the first thing
we will do today is write about
our summer vacations.
It should be done
in your neatest penmanship.
I want you to write
about everything you did
this summer."

Kelsey liked writing.
She began to write
as soon as Mrs. Vince gave her
a piece of paper.

She started her story
about the morning she woke up
to find her dog Goldie scratching
at the front door.
She wrote about finding a baby fawn
under the porch, shivering.
Kelsey took her time writing,
making sure she was using
her best penmanship.

"What's this?" said Mrs. Vince.
She stood next to Kelsey's desk,
reading what Kelsey had written.

"I'm writing about my fawn,"
said Kelsey. "The fawn we found
under our porch..."

"Kelsey," said Mrs. Vince.
"The assignment is to write
a true story
about your summer vacation.
This is not a time
to make up a story.
I will get you a new piece of paper,
and you will start over."

Josh was looking at Kelsey
from the next row.
Kelsey's eyes filled with tears.
"It is true," she whispered.
Kelsey started over
with a made-up story.
She wrote about a camping vacation
she wished she had gone on.

When Mrs. Vince came by,
she seemed much happier.
"Yes, good work,
Kelsey,"
she said.

Chapter 3
A Surprise for Mrs. Vince

Every day, Kelsey tried
to get her dad to let her stay home
from school.
Every day, her dad made her go.

One day, Mrs. Vince
told the girls and boys
about a special assignment
they would be working on.

"We are going to do
reports on animals,"
Mrs. Vince said.

"You will work with a partner.
You can choose any animal
that you want to learn about.
You will also do an art project
to go with your report.
It can be a poster or a diorama.
We will have an Animal Fair
and I will invite your families
to come in and visit.
You can present
your reports to everyone then."

At recess, Josh said,
"We can do a report
on deer. You have all those books
about deer and I have
a lot of information
from the Internet!"
Then Josh gave a big grin.
"And we can make a poster
with pictures of Baby."

"Good idea!" said Kelsey.
"We have lots
of pictures of Baby
that are so cute.
Mrs. Vince will be surprised."

Josh and Kelsey worked
on their deer report.
All the families of the children
in Mrs. Vince's class were invited
to the Animal Fair.

Josh and Kelsey
carefully put up their poster.
It was filled with pictures of Baby.
All the parents and Mrs. Vince
walked around the classroom
and listened to the children
talking about their projects.

The Deer Report

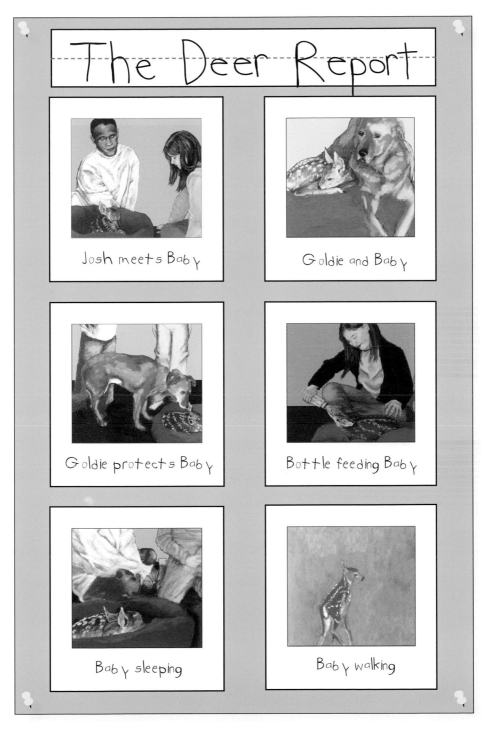

Josh meets Baby

Goldie and Baby

Goldie protects Baby

Bottle feeding Baby

Baby sleeping

Baby walking

When Mrs. Vince got to
Josh and Kelsey's table,
she stopped and her eyes widened.
"Oh," she said. "Oh!"
Her cheeks got pink.
"Oh, my," was all she said.

Kelsey's dad said,

"Didn't Kelsey tell you about the

little fawn we found

under our porch?

He is a special little guy.

Even our dog loves the fawn."

"Oh, my," was all Mrs. Vince

seemed to be able to say.

"Oh, my!"

After Mrs. Vince moved on
to the next table,
Josh and Kelsey looked
at each other and laughed.

"What's so funny?"
asked Kelsey's father.

"Oh, nothing!" they said.